Mount St. Helens
Volcano

Concept and Design: Robert D. Shangle
Text: Linda Kelso

First Printing September, 1980
Published by Beautiful America Publishing Company
P.O. Box 608, Beaverton, Oregon 97075
Robert D. Shangle, Publisher

ISBN 0-89802-209-6

Earth—Our Living, Changing Planet

Created by fire, sculpted by wind and water, our planet is ever changing and ever evolving. Indeed, it will continue to change—and be changed—as long as it exists.

It is easy to think of United States' land as finished and complete—to think the violent forces that change the earth must happen somewhere else—most likely in some primitive faraway place, and to people who are not nearly so civilized, who, like the land they live on, are still maturing.

Volcanoes—those fire-breathing mountains—inspire visions of leaping, twisting tongues of flaming lava thrust high into the air, only to fall and chase hapless innocents down mountainsides. Volcanoes stir up remembrances of myths and old movies of heroes rescuing fair maidens from witch doctors bent on appeasing angry gods with human sacrifices. Of the unfortunates buried at Pompeii, or in our own time, the rain of black ash on Surtsey. But a volcano in the United States—in 1980?

On May 18, 1980, Mount St. Helens, a beautiful cone-shaped peak in southwestern Washington state, 45 miles northeast of Portland, Oregon, erupted with such violence that its blast destroyed 156 square miles of timber in a fan-shaped swatch. Mudslides raced down the mountain's river valleys and tore out seven bridges along the Toutle River. The heat and force of the blast killed many people who were in the area—many of them camped far enough away that they fully expected to be safe from anything that occurred on the mountain. One-and-a-half cubic miles of the mountain were blown out: pulverized into rock, pebbles, ash, and dust. A mushroom-shaped cloud ascended to 63,000 feet and swept eastward, raining ash and other volcanic debris on most of three states.

Mount St. Helens was 9,677 feet high, a major peak of the Cascade Range in Washington state, a graceful cone sometimes called "The Fujiyama of the West," and almost always called "she"—a reference not at all related to her obviously feminine name, but to her distinctly feminine appearance, as compared to the glacier-carved, weathered shapes of other mountains.

Geologists knew her to be a volcano and had even predicted she would erupt sometime before the end of the 20th century. But they did not predict the immensity of what would happen when she did.

The May 18th eruption was one of the most powerful explosions ever witnessed by man—the largest explosion of the century in North America. Magma, hot molten rock, had collected in a pocket far beneath her. Volcanic gasses had accumulated in the magma, creating incredible pressure. The magma welled up inside the mountain, and finally the pressure could no longer be contained. No one alive today had ever witnessed such a blast. It tore asunder a mountain, casting the parts hundreds of miles away, ultimately to affect millions of lives, in one way or another.

For several hours of that once serene Sunday, hell broke out in that little corner of the earth. The dominions of Satan were spewed forth to incinerate everything—and everyone—in the way. It was an explosion akin to 50 large ocean freighters full of TNT, all going up at once, and more than 500 times as powerful as the atomic bomb dropped on Hiroshima at the end of the Second World War.

The cloud of ash, suspended in steam and gasses, rose to 63,000 feet above the mountain, through three layers of rain clouds, and swept north and east like an angry plague. It blackened the sky, turning day into night. Visibility fell to zero and electronically controlled street lights went on. Planes were grounded. Streets, roads, machinery, and lungs were soon clogged with the gritty, pervasive dust. A covering of ash, measured anywhere from feet to inches, soon accumulated beneath the route of the cloud. A DC-9 commercial aircraft, flying at 33,000 feet, flew four minutes through the ash cloud and was forced to land with clogged engines. Rail, air, and highway travelers were trapped throughout central and eastern Washington, Idaho, and Montana. Ultimately, 1,100 miles of highway in eastern Washington alone would be closed until the ash was removed.

Trees fell in the direction of the blast, flattened like so many toothpicks. Aerial photos bring to mind slivers of iron neatly lined up in the direction of magnetism. The once beautiful Spirit Lake disappeared in a massive avalanche of rock and mud.

Heat melted glacial ice and snow, and it cascaded downward, mixing with soil and ash. Mud, thus created, swept up everything in its path—rocks, timber, the artifacts of civilization—mixing and grinding it all into a churning mass that tumbled into valleys and thence into rivers.

The Toutle River and its tributaries drain the north and west flanks of the mountain. Into both the north and south forks of the Toutle went millions of tons of mud and debris. Timber, sucked up in the mud, floated to the top and rafted down the racing current, smashing into bridges. The growing mud flow rocketed down the river valley, cutting new channels, spilling over banks, gathering up still more debris. It spread out over low-lying areas, flooded campgrounds, logging camps, and homes. It caught up log trucks and smashed them around, tossing them to land, bent and broken, in heaps like so many children's toys abandoned in a thunderstorm.

A wall of mud surged on down the Toutle River Valley and knocked out every bridge for 30 miles. Hot ash and gasses warmed the water to probably over 90 degrees Fahrenheit in the immediate vicinity of the blast. The heat, and suspended debris, which literally smothered them, killed all the fish in the river.

The mud and silt was carried down the Toutle to the Cowlitz River and to the Columbia River. By Monday, May 19, the ocean-shipping channel in the Columbia, normally a minimum of 40 feet deep, was clogged with silt to about 18 feet, making ocean shipping impossible.

On the north face of the mountain, a pyroclastic flow—rock and ash suspended in hot gas—rushed down the side at possibly 100 miles per hour, incinerating everything in its path. Such a flow may be as hot as 1,500 degrees Fahrenheit.

Lightning, created by friction between the hot air of the blast and the surrounding cold air, crackled around the crater and about the summit. Along with hot ash, it started as many as 200 forest fires, many of which were smothered by ash. Others were left to burn as firefighters dared not come near. In weeks to come, Forest Service firefighters would attempt to extinguish blazes caused by smoldering timber buried in ash.

Mount St. Helens was left 1,277 feet shorter. Thirty-one people are known, or presumed to be, dead. Hundreds were left homeless, many jobless. At least 5,000 travelers had been stranded. Several major cities in central and eastern Washington, Idaho, and Montana were left to dig out of a coating of powdery, slick, fluid volcanic ash.

And a beautiful mountain was robed in black.

What is a Volcano?

The name volcano derives from the mythical Roman god, Vulcan, the god of fire and craftsmanship. Ancient peoples either feared or revered the volatile mountains as gods or the instruments of gods. Now we understand that our planet is continually building and changing—and volcanoes are one of the principal instruments of that change.

Scientists agree that the earth is comprised of a thin, 20-mile-deep crust of rock around a thick, 1,800-mile-deep mantle of fluid rock surrounding a dense, heavy iron core.

Most geologists now adhere to the theory that the crust is broken in a series of continent-sized plates that "float" on the molten mantle beneath them. The plates beneath the oceans differ, markedly, from those bearing continents. Oceanic plates are thinner, but denser and heavier than continental plates. The continually shifting plates move away from one another in some places and crash into each other elsewhere. It is where these plates collide that some of the geological violence, which produces earthquakes and volcanoes, occurs.

A volcano is a place where magma, molten rock from the interior of the earth, is expelled through a vent to the surface. When an oceanic plate and a continental plate collide, the thinner, heavier oceanic plate may plunge beneath the lighter continental plate. The leading edge of the sinking plate bends into the hot mantle below the crust and melts. On the underside of the continental plate is a series of chambers, hollow pockets into which magma rises. Gasses trapped in the magma expand, and when they do, great pressure builds in the chamber. Eventually, the pressure can no longer be contained, the magma erupts through the crust at a weak spot, and a volcano is born. The channel through which the eruption occurs is called a vent. Once a volcanic vent exists, magma from the chamber beneath it will usually continue to erupt through that vent when sufficient pressure builds to cause an eruption.

All volcanic eruptions are not violent. In fact, most volcanoes pop and sizzle at irregular intervals, and the truly cataclysmic, explosive eruptions occur infrequently enough to be notable.

And not all volcanoes are violent. Those of the Cascades are considered to be explosive—that is, they tend to erupt violently and sometimes explosively. But there is a second type of volcano, one from which a thinner, freer flowing lava extrudes almost continually, flowing away from the vent in long sheets. This type of extrusion builds a wide sloping mountain which, because it resembles an upturned warrior's shield when seen from the air, is called a shield volcano. Since the emanation of lava is comparatively constant, the kind of pressure that creates the explosive eruptions, for which volcanoes are famous, does not occur. Hawaii's Mauna Loa is a shield volcano.

Of the 529 known active volcanoes in the world today, 421 are located around the perimeter of the Pacific Ocean in what is commonly called the Ring of Fire. This circle of geological violence exists because the Pacific Ocean is spreading.

Volcanoes are not all bad, although sometimes their violent destruction is. They are the principal instruments of earth's recycling—the old rock and sediment gathered on the ocean floor, remelted to become the new land of tomorrow. They create new land that will become fertile farmland for agriculture; rugged peaks that shape the weather; calderas that cradle lovely lakes; hot water that is the source of potential geothermal energy; new river valleys, and fresh, new landscape to delight and challenge man.

Other Volcanoes

While volcanic activity around the world is continual, few explode with the violence evidenced by Mount St. Helens.

In the middle of the 15th century, B.C., the entire Minoan civilization, on an island in the Aegean Sea, abruptly vanished from the face of the earth. Scholars now believe its disappearance was attributable to the destruction wrought when Mt. Thera, on the island of Santorini some 70 miles distant, blew up. A layer of ash 100 feet thick is thought to have been left by this eruption.

One of history's most famous volcanic eruptions is that of Italy's Mount Vesuvius in 79 A.D. The city of Pompeii at its base was quickly buried in ash, but geologists now believe it was the nuée ardente, or glowing avalanche of gas-charged lava, that killed the Pompeiians. Such flows of debris, suspended in hot gasses, race down the sides of volcanoes in minutes, riding a cushion of compressed air.

A similar phenomenon killed the 30,000 inhabitants of the village of St. Pierre on Martinique in the West Indies. On May 8, 1902, in a violent eruption presaged by over two weeks of intense volcanic activity, a nuée ardente overcame the villagers in just minutes, leaving only one survivor, a prisoner who was confined in a cell with just one small window.

Krakatoa, a small island in the Sunda Strait between Java and Sumatra, is part of the Ring of Fire. Starting at 10:02 a.m. on August 27, 1883, in the most violent explosion recorded in modern history, Krakatoa pulverized itself. The eruption lasted two days, and the sound was eventually heard over 2,900 miles away. Some 300 towns were flooded by tidal waves and over 36,000 people killed. Fine dust encircled the earth and remained in the atmosphere for two years, creating magnificent sunsets. From the old caldera beneath the sea, into which the shell of mighty Krakatoa sank, rose Anak Krakatoa—''Child of Krakatoa''—a new island, indeed the child of the same force that destroyed the parent.

More recently, Siberia's Mt. Bezymianny expelled 2.4 billion tons of rock in March, 1956. Located in a sparsely inhabited part of the world, it affected few people and made little news.

Across the world, volcanism built a new island under the watchful eyes of science. In late 1963 the island of Surtsey was born in the Atlantic Ocean near Iceland.

And near the village of Paricutin, 200 miles west of Mexico City, farmers watched as a new volcanic cone rose from a small opening in a cornfield. In a week the cone had risen to 500 feet, and five months later it was 1,200 feet above the surrounding land. For nine years, from 1943 through 1952, Mt. Paricutin continued its building. In the process a lava flow buried a nearby town.

A discussion of other volcanoes would not be complete without mention of North America's Lassen Peak. Southernmost peak in the Cascades, until the Mount St. Helens eruption, it was the contiguous states' most recent active volcano. From 1914 through 1921, Lassen Peak frequently pelted the neighborhood with ash and itself with lava in an incredible number of *observed* eruptions. No one knows how many minor steam and ash explosions occurred, since the weather in this region, being what it is during the winter, caused the mountain to be obscured and such activity was never recorded. A major, lateral blast, in many ways similar to Mount St. Helens', if not as violent, took place on May 22, 1915. After 65 years the ''Devastated Area'' still shows the effects of that major eruption.

Her Past

The high peaks of the Cascade Range in Washington, Oregon, and northern California are all of volcanic origin. Including British Columbia's Mt. Garibaldi, there are 17 snow-capped mountains known to be volcanoes in this chain—all recognized as dormant rather than extinct. That is to say—any *could* become active again. But while there is evidence of current volcanic activity on most of these mountains, it was Mt. St. Helens that caught the attention of geologists as the Cascade peak most likely to erupt soon.

The composite cone, which forms Mount St. Helens today, may be only 1,000 years old. It is an accumulation of successive deposits of ash and lava—the products of regular volcanic activity. This youthful peak sits astride the remains of a much older ancestor, whose age is gauged to be at least 35,000 years. That ancient volcano seems to have been extremely volatile. The products of its eruptions have been identified hundreds of miles away. One of these products is pumice, which emerges during an eruption as frothy lava filled with gas bubbles and hardens quickly around the bubbles—somewhat like a rock of Swiss cheese. St. Helens was sometimes called the place where rocks float, because of the extensive accumulations of pumice. In fact, some pumice does float because it is so thoroughly laced with bubbles that it is lighter than water.

During the early days of the present mountain, some 2,000 years ago before the cone began to form, streams of ropy lava called pahoehoe flowed from a vent on the south side and hardened quickly, leaving tunnels in the flow—the lava caves for which St. Helens is known.

The several Indian tribes that lived in the St. Helens region called the mountain, variously, "Lady of Fire," "Person From Whom Smoke Comes," "Fire Mountain," or some other name referring to smoke and fire. She figured in their legends as an old witch who had been transformed into a raving beauty, or as a woman angry with her two lovers, Mount Hood and Mount Adams. She kept the sacred fire, and the people came from all directions to borrow it.

Captain George Vancouver named the peak Mount St. Helens on May 19, 1792 in honor of Alleyne Fitzherbert, the Baron St. Helens, who had recently executed an important treaty with Spain.

Early settlers in Washington and Oregon posted many accounts of Mount St. Helens' activity during the 1800s. Geologists cannot entirely reconcile reported dates with geologic evidence, but it seems that a period of activity commenced in approximately 1832, built to a rather large eruption in 1842, and then diminished until all activity ceased in 1857. During the 1842 eruption, a French-Canadian voyageur reported that the light was so bright he could see to pick up a pin at midnight.

More recently in 1928, steam was observed on the south side near the summit.

By 1980 the scars left from the eruptions of the 1800s had healed over, and the young mountain reigned over the southern Washington Cascades with queenly elegance. St. Helens wore a raimant of pristine snow the year round. Her upper slopes were cluttered with pumice rubble in contrast to the rambling meadows found on many other alpine peaks. In her forests, life was abundant.

Herds of Roosevelt Elk and blacktailed deer, the elusive bobcat and cougar, charming raccoons and lumbering black bear made their homes on the ridges and in the valleys. Her lakes and rivers were rich with fish—the Toutle River was said to be one of the finest salmon and steelhead tributaries in the country.

Spirit Lake was kidney-shaped, trapped behind a dam

formed of mudslides from past eruptions. Sunk in a glacial depression, it was a young lake whose water had immersed giant Douglas firs. When the wind howled down the canyon and through the trees, it moaned. Perhaps that eerie sound contributed to the Indian belief that spirits inhabited the lake.

Bounded by tall firs in the clear, high-country air, the lake, and its environs, was a delightful destination of hundreds of campers and backpackers. Three major youth organizations maintained camps at the lake, and there were four developed public campgrounds to serve the thousands of northwesterners and tourists from around the world who visited the exquisite lake and intriguing mountain. Radiating from Spirit Lake, an extensive trail system penetrated the back country and provided access to several small, high lakes. Spring brought a profusion of wildflowers, summer a restful respite from civilization's hustle and bustle, and in the brisk autumn, hunters trudged the hills and dales seeking game. The winter snowpack attracted cross-country skiers and only the hardiest of downhillers, for there was no developed ski area at Mount St. Helens. Climbers sought her slopes at all times of the year, for the climb, while not difficult, was exhilerating. And the view from the summit was worth the effort—Mount Rainier and Mount Baker to the north, Mount Adams to the east; Mount Hood, the Sisters and Jefferson in the south.

Mount St. Helens was the crown jewel of the Gifford Pinchot National Forest, even though the very top of her summit was owned by the Burlington Northern Railroad.

And, some people believe, in her remote valleys lived the legendary Sasquatch, or Bigfoot.

Prelude

Earthquakes are a fairly common occurrence where two plates of the earth's crust meet. So the one that was recorded at 3:47 p.m. on March 20, 1980 was not necessarily of particular note, other than it was centered near Mount St. Helens.

But volcanologists had been studying this mountain, and in 1975 they had predicted that it would erupt sometime within a century—maybe even before the end of this one. So when additional quakes occurred, the scientists were intrigued. Perhaps the quakes presaged volcanic activity. But they hesitated to make too much of it. The public is not fond of false alarms.

They did not have to postpone a decision long. Just a week later on March 27, shortly after noon, an airborne radio newsman gave the first notice that Mt. St. Helens was erupting. In a brief puff, the mountain sent up the first in a series of ash and steam eruptions.

When that eruption was over, there was a new crater carved through the blanket of ice at the mountain's summit and into the rock beneath. It was about the size of a football field and roughly 100 feet deep. A light coating of ash blackened the snow around the crater.

Succeeding ash and steam eruptions created a second crater about 30 feet from the first one, then merged the two into a yawning chasm.

Geologists explained these initial eruptions amounted to the mountain clearing its throat. In the 123 years since previous volcanic activity, ice and rock had fallen into the conduit and plugged it up. Pressure in the magma below the mountain was seeking release. That first ash was simply old rock, pulverized by the force which blasted it out; the steam was simply ground water heated by rising temperatures in the vent. While there was a possibility of a lava eruption, geologists would not go so far as to say there *would* be one. In fact, in the early days of the first eruptions, the major concern was mudslides. Mount St. Helens had several glaciers and a winter snow pack. Volcanic heat could cause the snow and glaciers to melt rapidly and cause avalanches and mudslides.

Officials, without specific guidance from science, opted for caution. In early April a restricted zone was imposed around the peak and no one without specific authorization was permitted to be within that zone. In fact, restriction was hard to enforce. The whole area was crisscrossed by logging roads and a lot of people who lived there were intimately familiar with the network. Since it was physically impossible to barricade every road, it was impossible to keep everyone out.

It was not surprising that on at least two occasions the adventuresome climbed the heaving peak. On April 3 a solitary climber reached the top. He reported a strong sulphur odor and ash ten feet deep at the edge of the crater. A party of three had just made the summit early in the morning of April 13 when a steam and ash eruption, lasting approximately 20 minutes, bubbled up. They were fortunate that the wind carried the eruption away from them.

A week after that first eruption another phenomenon occurred—harmonic tremors. A harmonic tremor is a different kind of earthquake. The usual earthquake causes a sudden sharp jolt and fractures rock. By contrast, harmonic tremors are more like waves in the earth's surface and can be likened to a vibrato. Some people say the best way to visualize a tremor is to imagine the earth's crust as a bowl of shaking gelatin. The tremors, said the scientists, were most likely evidence that magma was moving beneath Mount St. Helens.

And then there was the bulge. Early in April it was noted that the north face of the mountain was bulging out. That bulge eventually reached out about 500 feet

Mt. St. Helens from Yale Lake, photographed in September of 1979.
Note that the pictures on pages 20 and 25 complete a series of before,
during, and after shots taken from the same locatin.

*The north side of Mt. St. Helens, photographed during the previous winter.
This is the side of the mountain that blew out in the May 18 eruption.
(Following pages) Mt. St. Helens as photographed from its northwest
side in January of 1980.*

*Mt. St. Helens as photographed from the Portland Rose Gardens,
summer of 1979.*

Early morning sun on Mt. St. Helens, photographed in the fall of 1979 from Portland.

Mt. St. Helens photographed from Yale Lake on the south side, during the first series of eruptions that began March 27, 1980.

This photo was taken from the east side of the mountain, looking west, in early April. It shows the increasing size of the crater.

The results of the first series of eruptions, showing the beginning crater as photographed on the north side. It was this side of Mt. St. Helens that completely blew out in the May 18 eruption.

17

A helicopter ventures into the ever-enlarging crater during the latter part of April.

Photographed on Saturday, May 17, the day before the major eruption, from the south side.

(Following page) The May 18 major eruption photographed from Yale Lake. Note that the pictures on pages 9 and 25 complete a series of before, during and after shots taken from the same location.

The devastation created by the May 18 eruption.
(Previous page) May 18 eruption as photographed from the south side
of the mountain.

The devastated area north of the mountain as photographed July 24, 1980.
The foreground is looking into the blown-out portion of the mountain.

Part of the devastated area approximately 12 miles north of the crater.

Mt. St. Helens from Yale Lake on July 2, 1980. Note that the pictures on pages 9 and 20 complete a series of before, during and after shots taken from the same location.

Late day sun plays upon the mountain in the latter part of July.

Part of the devastated area photographed on June 30, 1980.

Photographed from the north si

, with Mt. Hood in the background.

The devastation following the May 18, 1980 eruption.

The mountain at sunset, July 29, 1980.

The May 18 major eruption fro

...e south side of the mountain.

July 26, 1980, photographed from the north.

The Toutle River near I-5. Note the height of the ash on the tree, left by flooding from the May 18 eruption.

A portion of Spirit Lake two months after the May 18 eruption.

July 29, 1980.

Looking toward Mt. Rainier on June 30, 1980. This photo is taken from the same location as page 39.

June 30, 1980. Looking toward Mt. St. Helens from the west.
This photo is taken from the same location as page 38.

Photographed July 29, 1980 near the rim of the crater. Mt. Adams
is in the background.

July 22 eruption as photographed from Oregon.

Photographed July 27, 1980 from the northeast, showing the devastated portions of the area to the north of the mountain. Spirit Lake is in the right-hand portion of the picture.

A cloud cover invades the mountain, June 17, 1980.

Photograph taken July 27, 1980 in the late day shows the blown-out portion of the mountain.

Photographed June 30, 1980 from the south side, looking north.
Mt. Rainier is in the background.

Late evening photograph shows the cracks in the forming dome and the lava underneath.

The dome developing inside of the crater, July 19, 1980.

47

Mt. St. Helens photographed from the west, July 2, 1980.

July 29, photographed from the northeast.

July 26, 1980 at sunset, looking into the crater.

Looking over the rim of the crater July 26, 1980.

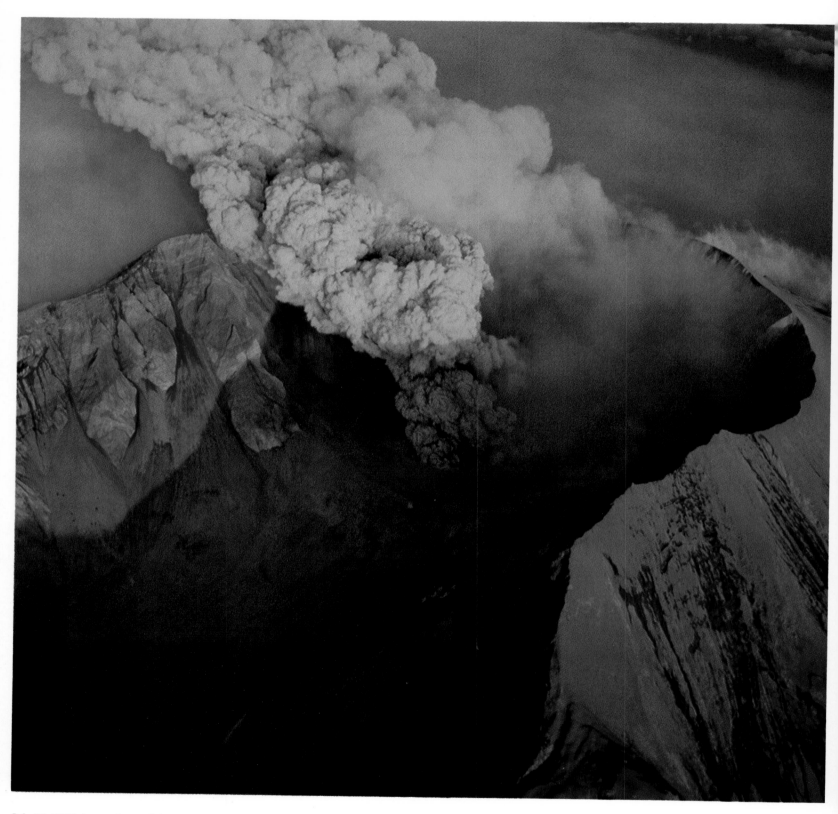

July 22, 1980, latter phases of the eruption at sunset.

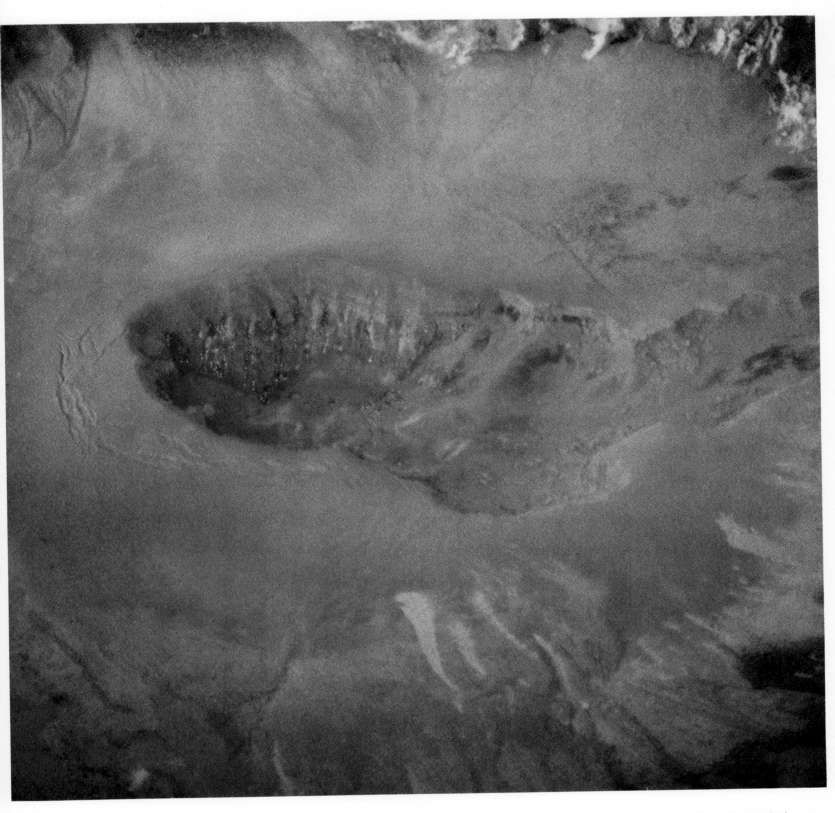

Molten lava inside the crater.

July 22 eruption photographed from the south side.
Mt. Rainier is in the background.

July 22 eruption, photographed from Portland.

from its starting point, having increased at the incredible rate of five feet a day in early May. That, said the geologists, might be caused by magma welling up inside the mountain—but again, no one was sure. But as the bulge increased, it seemed only a matter of time until it broke off in a massive slide. And that was a clear and imminent danger—not to be challenged.

Meanwhile, people who lived near Mount St. Helens found the novelty of a real, live volcano in the backyard wearing off and the assorted inconveniences imposed by the situation became more noticeable. Particularly affected were the loggers who could not go to work. People who had property in the restricted area could not go to it, and a few who had businesses in the red zone had to close them. Teams of geologists set up instruments to measure any changes, no matter how minute, and scientists and the press swarmed over the mountain recording and reporting its every burp. An air of expectancy hung over the small communities around Mount St. Helens, but no one knew what to expect or when to expect it.

The people who had homes at or on the way to Spirit Lake became restless. The scouts had already managed to get much of the gear out of their camps, and the homeowners wanted to do the same. The world was captivated by the 84-year-old man who refused to leave his lodge, saying his mountain would never harm him. He received a special dispensation from the $500 fine assessed against anyone found in the red zone who wasn't supposed to be there.

Some people sloughed off warnings of danger. It somehow seemed inconceivable that anything approaching the kind of disaster some scientists said *could* happen ever would. Others, more cautious, did what was feasible to heed warnings as they were issued, placing faith in science and its practitioners to interpret the mountain's unusual behavior.

As April waned, eruptive activity waned, although quakes and tremors continued. In early May, after 16 relatively ''quiet'' days, a quake measured at 5.0 on the Richter scale shook the mountain, and soon the steam and ash eruptions began anew. The once white slopes of the peak were draped in grey ash, and at the summit there was a massive crater.

The restless Spirit Lake area property owners petitioned the governor for permission to enter the red zone. The harried official finally relented, and on May 17, escorted by police, a caravan of property owners drove to the lake. They had four hours in the red zone and a promise of four more hours the next day. No one was permitted to stay overnight.

Mt. St. Helens and the Fremont Bridge, photographed from the Vista Street Bridge, in Portland.

May 18, 1980

May 18 dawned clear and calm. Nothing exceptional was going on to give note that a major eruption was in sight. No larger than usual quakes occurred. No preliminary burst of steam. No slipping and sliding of the monstrous bulge. No auxiliary shots of debris. No lava. No rise in temperature.

A dedicated geologist, camped some five miles north of the peak, reported to his base in Vancouver that nothing was new.

Up in the Green River valley, over 15 miles north and a few ridges away, some campers got up to start their breakfast.

Two geologists and their pilot were flying over the mountain in a small plane. It was a thrilling experience—their first close look at a subject dear to them. They probably hoped the mountain would do something for them.

It did.

That pilot may have been the first person to give notice to the world of the incredible explosion that wracked the mountain. He reported to Air Traffic Control that the whole north side of the mountain "just went."

At 8:31 a.m. a quake shook the mountain. The bulge on the north face slid away and out of the opening rolled a cloud of ash and steam. Right behind that came tremendously hot gasses, the incredible pressure trapped in the magma chamber below the mountain was finally released, to explode like the granddaddy of all pressure cookers.

This practically instantaneous release of enormous pressure created a shock wave that surged down valleys and up over ridges carrying ash, steam, mud, and rock. The wind reached hurricane force—almost 200 miles an hour.

By May 18th St. Helens' eruptions must have been routine to the air traffic controllers. They asked the pilot if he could give an estimate of how much of the mountain was gone, then asked him for verification when he told them, "the whole side."

The explosion made a bang heard as far away as Vancouver, British Columbia, Canada, 225 miles north. It continued all day in successive billows of purple-blue clouds, which look in photos like so much purple cauliflower.

Within ten minutes commercial pilots in the air near the billowing cloud reported that they couldn't accurately estimate the breadth and height of the plume. It was described by the usually laconic pilots as incredible, spectacular. They told Air Traffic Control that they were seeing a great deal of lightning.

Responsible agencies scrambled to get observers in the air and rescue equipment on the ground. By early afternoon Army helicopters were flying low over the Toutle River Valley, searching for survivors. Unable to see through the clouds to know just what was occurring on the mountain, pilots and their crews risked their lives to rescue several stranded people—and to give word to the world of the enormity of what had happened. The chopper crews alerted the state patrol to the wall of mud surging down the Toutle Valley, and probably many lives were saved because it was possible to evacuate threatened people in time.

Those animals still alive stood stunned and in shock. A cataclysm had occurred that would profoundly affect the lives of hundreds of people and hundreds of thousands of other living things.

Mere numbers—dollars, statistics, hours, weeks, and years—cannot tell the story. The story is in the people and their land, and how both will never be the same again.

The Survivors

The little dramas of life are the big stories of people caught in events not of their own making. Thirty-one people are known to have died in the May 18 eruption; another 34 are still unaccounted for. But there were some people in the Mount St. Helens area that morning for whom the clock had not yet run out.

An elderly man and his four dogs sat out the inferno in their cabin ten miles southwest of the blast. They were flown out 13 days later unharmed.

A party of six, two women, two men, and two teenage boys were camped on a ridge north of the cone, five miles out of the red zone. At the first puffs of the fatal explosion they were delighted. They had a perfect view through the saddle of an intervening ridge. Then they saw the massive explosion. At first it looked like a baseball, then it broadened out. The mountain disappeared as they watched. Then they heard a roaring sound, which got louder and louder. They could see trees being uprooted as the force of the blast raced toward them. It took the shock wave less than a minute to reach them.

At that point they scrambled into one of their two vehicles, abandoning a pickup truck, all the camping equipment, and some clothing. At speeds up to 60 miles per hour, they raced the car down the narrow, winding logging road. One person remembers feeling the heat on the back of his neck. On the way they saw other campers, blissfully unaware about the hell that was about to engulf them. Hurricane-force winds caught up with the speeding, bouncing car, and the sky darkened. Heat lightning added to the netherworld scenario. The fact that the road crossed a logged out area probably saved the car from being smashed under falling trees. As they neared the paved road, blobs of mud coated the car. Finally, at the highway the mud gave way to ash, and they sped to safety.

Southward, a young couple was camped by the Toutle River. The water rose so fast that they climbed to the top of their car to escape. The car was knocked loose, and the frightened pair was dumped into a swirling maelstrom of logs. Almost trapped among the churning wood, the two scrambled out. Rescuers waded through mud up to their chests in order to reach the pair.

Six campers, 30 air miles from the mountain, awoke to find trees toppling about them. With no warning, two of them found themselves buried in ash and timber. They couldn't see and didn't know what was happening. Frantically digging and clawing, it took them ten minutes to hew their way to an embattled world under night-black sky. Of the four friends who were with them, two were not to be seen again. Leaving two badly injured friends in a shack, the man and woman began a 15-mile hike to rescue. A helicopter returned to ferry out the injured.

Three loggers were working in the blast zone. Burned over large parts of their bodies by hot ash and cinders, two of them hiked eight miles through choking dust, in miserable pain, before being found.

Elsewhere, a young family, parents and two daughters, one aged four and the other an infant, had backpacked to a campsite along the Green River trail. The woman remembers a low rumbling, then rapid air pressure changes that made their ears pop repeatedly. The sky turned black, as ash began to bury the campsite. No fast escape could be attempted with two small children, so the family found refuge in an abandoned shack. It was small protection from the holocaust, but it provided shelter from the rain of debris.

That night the family stayed in their tent, and in the morning sought to reach their car. Trails had been obliterated in the dust and fallen trees blocked the way.

The four lived on survival food, carried in their backpacks, and were thankful for a small spring where they could get fresh water.

By noon they became worried. How would they get out? A rescue chopper buzzing overhead seemed unaware that they were there. But the pilot did spot them, and was astonished to see people alive on the dead land. He was unable to land right at that area, but sent rescuers in on foot to escort the survivors to a safer landing spot.

And the pair of geologists and their pilot, delightedly snapping pictures on several passes around the mountain, may well be the last people alive today to have seen Spirit Lake. Air Traffic Control asked the pilot if he would like to turn back to take another look. "Negative," he replied. Diving to increase airspeed, the little craft sped south to safety. Those aboard it had missed destruction by less than a second.

The fate of many of the people who are unaccounted for may never be known. One of them is the 84-year-old man who refused to leave his beloved mountain. Where he and his cats had made their home is now covered with tons of mud.

And the last that is known of the intense, young geologist is his final call, an excited, not frightened, "Vancouver, Vancouver, this is it!"

The Shattered Land

Where once the rolling hills and ridges were carpeted with fir forests, there is now a barren wasteland. Where once clear mountain streams gurgled over eroded pebbles, there is mud. Where once loggers worked the forests, they now attempt to clear away enough debris to reach the billion board feet of downed timber, some of which may be salvageable.

Where once there were homes in which people lived and vacationed, there are now shells of buildings ripped from their foundations and deposited askew in the mud. Where there was a two-lane highway to Spirit Lake, there is now rubble.

And 1,277 feet of the top of the mountain is gone. Where there used to be a graceful snow-covered cone, there is a squat black butte. Someone commented that the mountain looks as though a third of its top had been neatly sliced off with a giant cleaver.

A huge crater is left—shaped like a giant amphitheater, it measures a mile by two miles and is 3,000 feet deep, open to the north.

Cities in the path of the ash cloud were left with the challenge of how to get rid of tons of ash, which covered them like snow.

Eastern Washington is an important agricultural area. Volcanic ash deposits eventually became rich, fertile land for crops. But ash deposited on the crops themselves is something else. There is no body of scientific study to aid the farmers in dealing with effects of the ash, so the net effect of the blanket of ash cast upon young crops cannot even be predicted. What happens to the equipment used to plant, nurture, and harvest those crops is easily learned. The abrasive ash works on metal like sandpaper on wood. Farmers face the peril of bringing the crops to maturity despite the ash, then being unable to harvest them because of the danger of ruining expensive equipment.

Thirty-three ships were at dock at the several ports above the confluence of the Cowlitz and Columbia rivers, where the ship channel was most seriously clogged with ash and debris. Some of them were unable to leave the harbors for several weeks. Others waited far down the Columbia until the river was dredged sufficiently so they could pass.

It could take an army of statisticians years to assess the damage—which cannot be entirely measured in statistics anyway. How does one put a dollar value on the swallows that starved to death because ash had killed off all the insects on which they feed?

Is there any way to measure the inconveniences imposed on almost everyone who lives and works anywhere near Mount St. Helens?

Where once a river teemed with fish, there is barely a river left. The glacial ice, which fed it, has all melted. How does one measure the hours and minutes of fishing in a favorite spot, never more to be had. What, if anything, can be done for animals who have lost their homes?

In truth the effects of Mount St. Helens' eruption will continue to be felt in many ways for a long, long time.

Postlude

What does a mountain do for an encore? If it is Mount St. Helens, it goes right on erupting, albeit with not so much enthusiasm.

Less than two weeks after the huge May 18 eruption, on May 25, a new cloud of steam and ash was emitted. This second eruption sent a cloud to 20,000 feet, and cities to the south and west got their first taste of volcanic ash. That very light dusting had hardly been swept up when, on June 12, late in the evening, Mount St. Helens went off again. People in southwest Washington and northwest Oregon awoke on Friday, June 13, to their first real taste of more than just a little bit of ash. While the total accumulation probably did not exceed 1/16 of an inch, the Oregonians could now feel sympathy for the plight of their less fortunate neighbors in Washington, still trying to get rid of the May 18 crop of ash.

Meanwhile, during the first few days after the May 18 explosion, the battered properties along the Toutle faced a new threat. A 200-foot-high, 17-mile-long earthen dam had been emplaced at the outlet of Spirit Lake. Water quickly rose behind it, and geologists feared the dam would not hold. Residents were allowed to visit their homes for very brief periods under the watchful escort of law enforcement personnel. Within a week the water level dropped. Apparently the dam would hold.

Regardless of the risk, scientists flocked to the devastated area to look and learn. They found a dead land. Portions of the area around Spirit Lake were buried under as much as 400 feet of ash. On May 22 the water temperature in the lake was 92 degrees Fahrenheit; on June 1 the lake measured from 75 to 100 feet deep, and the temperature had risen to 97 degrees on the surface, 95 degrees on the bottom.

Harried geologists, sated with new data to chew on, still could not predict what the mountain would do next. They did predict that a lava dome would build in the crater, since in the past this was a customary aftermath of this kind of eruption. The continually cloudy weather made visual observation spotty, but radar imagery presented a continuing coverage of what was happening in the crater.

On May 30 the mountain fulfilled the prediction. A lava dome was beginning to build on top of the vent. What was happening, said the scientists, was that lava was welling up through the conduit and solidifying when chilled by the cold air. As more lava was extruded, it would push up from beneath, building the dome from the bottom. Observers looked in vain for a red glow, evidence of lava running into the crater from under the dome.

Periodic puffs of steam and ash continued as did harmonic tremors and earthquakes. Heavy clouds blanketed the area, making visual observation difficult, but the volcano's activities were monitored both by radar and high-flying, specially equipped aircraft.

So many scientists, reporters, and photographers sought entrance to the endangered area that a committee was appointed to screen these requests. Each party to enter the area would be required to maintain radio contact at all times, and no member was to travel farther than a fifteen-minute hike from the vehicle.

The dome kept growing. On June 21 it was more than 200 feet high and over 600 feet wide. A week later it was astonishing the scientists, growing 80 feet a day. All over the floor of the massive crater were hundreds of fumaroles. A cloud of steam hung over the mountain almost all the time. The air above it reeked with sulphur. News stories reported that anywhere from 50 to 1,300 tons of sulfur dioxide a day were being emitted from the mountain.

Geologists became concerned that the dome was plugging the vent, which would allow pressure to build again and precipitate another eruption. They were right. On July 22 pressure shattered the lava dome, sending its fragments flying and an ash cloud 11 miles up. It was the second largest eruption and was followed in quick succession by two more major and three minor eruptions before the evening was over. Ash again drifted east, dusting the same beleaguered Washington communities again. This eruption was estimated at around 700 feet in diameter. Glowing rocks were visible within the new crater, and this, it was said, indicated the temperature within the vent could be as much as 13,000 degrees Fahrenheit.

On August 7 Mt. St. Helens erupted again. There was a cloud sent up to over 44,000 feet and a pyroclastic flow. But this time scientists said they may have determined how to predict it. They said the nature of preceding quakes, harmonic tremors, and ratio of gasses being vented have established an identifiable pattern. Four hours before the blast, an alert was sounded. All loggers working in the area, scientists, reporters, and residents were given ample warning to evacuate.

As summer wanes and autumn rains become imminent, builders work against time to construct earthen walls to retain the mass of debris in the Toutle Valley. The rain is expected to run off the compacted, cement-like ash very quickly and create massive flooding conditions.

If Mount St. Helens remains true to its past patterns of eruptive activity, northwesterners can expect a long siege. The last period of volcanic activity lasted 15 years. With the novelty beginning to wear off, people in the area feel a little weary of the volcano and its antics. What it has done and what it will do will determine much of the way of life of its people, who are learning to live with a volcano.

Epilogue

In an instant a swatch of land reaching 15 miles from the center of the blast, some of western United States' most lovely mountain countryside, was transformed. Today it is the land of Hades brought to life—in death.

Wind alone knocks down and batters whatever it hits. Heat alone incinerates. Flying debris—sand, gravel, rock—abrade and demolish. If a combination of all three visited with no warning, all living things would cease to be.

What color is death? It is grey. Grey land, grey sky, grey water.

The sound of death is silence. Imagine the surface of the moon: there is no air to carry sound waves. Then imagine that kind of silence. Imagine a land so barren and sterile nothing is growing on it. Imagine everything, no matter what it was, how big it was, how strong it was—destroyed.

For science there is a laboratory. How does nature start from scratch? Think of the persistence of the little things that will come to inhabit the sterile land—life so tiny that we can't see it. Life that will begin the transformation which will in turn make the land habitable for larger creatures that will follow. Think of the creatures who will make what homes they can on the still shuddering mountain—a testimony to the tenacity of nature and her creatures to build and renew with no regret.

Seeing is believing—but do you really want to see it? You want to remember it as it was, the captivating Spirit Lake, the invigorating climb to Norway Pass, the mists on the trails in the back country, the little lakes nestled in granite depressions. The Plains of Abraham, worth every huff and puff to get there for cross-country skiing. The mystery of Bigfoot. The crater filled with sparkling snow, blushing in the early morning sun at the end of the daybreak climb.

The view of Mount Rainier, rising majestically in the north, the lodges and campgrounds and trails and trees and flowers. A mountain with a mystique.

It's all gone.

It will never again be what we remember in our lifetime—or in the lifetimes of many generations of our descendants. The Mount St. Helens that our great-great grandchildren will know will be vastly different than it was before or is today. Here we have a volcanic showcase, a living laboratory where man can observe what happens to the land after it has been wiped clean and nature starts over.

The curious will flock to see—and be awed. Scientists from around the world will come to study the havoc wrought and, as the years pass, the exciting birth and development of a new biological community on the virgin land.

The eruption, and what it did, is the basis of which legends will be born. It is our reminder that man cannot control nature. He never has and probably never will—and perhaps should not want to.

Mt. St. Helens, 1980—and end—and a beginning.

$6.95

ISBN 0-89802-209-